HOW TO MAKE PEOPLE
REALLY FEEL LOVED

How to Make People Really Feel Loved

and Other Life-Giving Observations

CHARLIE W. SHEDD

SERVANT PUBLICATIONS
ANN ARBOR, MICHIGAN

Vine Books is an imprint of Servant Publications especially designed to serve evangelical
Christians.

Unless otherwise noted, Scripture verses are from the Revised Standard Version of the Bible,
© 1946, 1952, 1971 by the Division of Christian Education of the National Council of
Churches of Christ in the USA. Used by permission. In addition to the primary translations,
occasional quotations from Scripture have been used from the following translations of the
Bible, as noted below. All rights reserved by the original copyright holder:

NAB:	New American Bible
NASB:	New American Standard Bible
TLB:	Living Bible
KJV:	King James Version
NIV:	New International Version
GNB:	Good News Bible

The names of all those mentioned in this book have been changed to protect their privacy.

Cover photo: © Michael Pole/Westlight. Used by permission.

Printed in the United States of America.
ISBN 1-56955-013-0

Contents

God is love

and his dream

is to establish

a bond of universal love

on which he can build his Kingdom

and reign forever.

If we love one another, God lives

in union with us, and His love is

made perfect in us.

1 John 4:12, GNB

A new commandment I give unto you,

That ye love one another;

as I have loved you....

By this shall all men know

that ye are my disciples,

if ye have love one to another.

JOHN 13:34-35, KJV

ONE

How to Make People
Really Feel Loved

Let all that you do be done in love.
1 CORINTHIANS 16:14

*Withhold not good from them to whom it is due,
when it is in the power of thine hand to do it.*

PROVERBS 3:27, KJV

One of the wisest men I ever knew was a big Swede who never finished high school. Why? Because things were tough in the old country, so he came to Minnesota. Could he make a living in the United States?

When I knew him he had became one of America's top construction superintendents. He supervised the building of what were then our country's tallest skyscrapers. And he took great pride in his finished product. Every one of his buildings was a true giant, with the forever look.

But he was even more proud of another thing—*he was a master at making other people feel extra special.*

I watched him as he worked with his men. Laborer, water boy, trained engineer, president of the company, no difference. After a few words with him, they all seemed to stand straighter, walk taller—and look at the smiles!

Up and down the halls of our church I watched him too. Here I saw him as a genius with boys, girls, men, women. And oh, how the ladies loved him. They gathered around him like hummingbirds. Why? Because he had a good word for each and every one.

One day the Big Swede and I were on a trip. This was the time to ask him more about his people secrets. So he gave me a lecture on people-dealing, and it was one great lecture.

"On the day I left home," he began, "my father said to me, 'Son, I'm sorry you did not get a good book-learning. But you know how poor we've been. OK, so you've got to make up for that some way, and now I will tell you how.

'There is an old proverb you must learn and live by. My father taught it to me. His father taught it to him, and it has been a long time with us in our family. This is how it goes:

Even an ass likes to think he is worthy
to be quartered with the king's horses!

'You study that, son, and I promise it will be even better than the schools for you. You will see. Learning that—and living by it—will close even the biggest gaps in everything you do.'

"So all the way to America, I studied about that.

"What I decided it meant is that even the plainest person likes to hope he is somebody special. Alright, I would train myself to imagine what other people see when they look in the mirror. And my father was right. It did close the gaps.

"This is not easy," he warned, "because you've got to break the habit of thinking of yourself first. But if you can turn your mind in this direction, you will discover there really is something special in every person. And the more you practice looking for the good in others, the more you will see it quick."

Then he concluded his discourse with this gem:

"The secret is to find the good things and to give them back. I mean out loud, sincere, and very strong. If you will do this and keep on till it comes easy, then another beautiful thing happens. One day you'll begin to really love people like the Bible says you should."

I'm glad he made that last point. Without a real love at the source, a divine love, our words will not ring true. There is a chattery flattery which is strictly phoney. But that's not for us. For us, loving with integrity is an admonition straight from the Lord.

Prayer for every day—
Lord, help me to love every man, every woman,
every child, with your love…. Amen

TWO

Do You REALLY Love Yourself?

Let another praise you, and not your own mouth;
a stranger, and not your own lips.

PROVERBS 27:2

*F*aithful are the wounds
of a friend....

PROVERBS 27:6

Yu Pin Wong was my roommate in college. He was fresh from China, and "Yupi" fast became a favorite with all of us.

But sometimes life was downright uncomfortable living with this Chinese philosopher. By one simple sentence he could divest me of my facades. Somehow he could see a side of me no one else could see.

Ah, Yupi, so often you left me feeling terribly exposed.

Yet in how many ways you blessed me, too. Like for instance, your letter on self-effacement. I still have it. I still read it on occasion, and it still blesses me.

I quote:

> Dear Cholly:
>
> Today I take my pen in hand to write you careful word. Many times you say, "Yu Pin, I really not so good as you think."
>
> You very humble fellow, Cholly. But when you say these things I have feeling you want me say, "You more better than anyone."
>
> What is the matter? In my country I am taught, "Humility only come from good opinion of self." I am happy with your friendship. I feel you are nice people. But what you feel?
>
> I think you need like Cholly better until you do not worry so much how good he is.
>
> Your missing companion,
> Yu Pin

Do you ever catch yourself maneuvering your back into a position to be patted? Or flapping your ears unduly for an encouraging word? I do. God must have known this would happen to some of us. Why else would the Bible have so much to say about genuine humility? Why else would he have given me a roommate like Yupi?

So what's the answer to this tricky business of self-effacement? One answer comes back loud and clear:

What matters most is affirmation from the Lord.

Lord, help me to love you better
So I can love Cholly better,
To love all the people
In all the world better. Amen.

THREE

Getting Even—
God's Way

Never pay back evil for evil to anyone. Respect what is right in the sight of all men. If possible, so far as it depends on you, be at peace with all men. Never take your own revenge, beloved... for it is written, "Vengeance is Mine, I will repay," says the Lord.

ROMANS 12:17-19, NASB

*Let all bitterness and wrath and anger...
be put away from you, with all malice...
forgiving one another,
as God in Christ forgave you.*

EPHESIANS 4:31-32

S hirley D. lived in a large Midwestern city. She was assistant manager of a fashionable employment agency. She had been active in our church youth group, so we were good friends. Now she was sharing with me from the depths of her soul:

Dear Dr. Shedd:

Last week something happened which I must tell you about. You remember that terrible experience I had when Jean J. blackballed me from her sorority? The boy she liked rather liked me, so she was out to get me. I was so broken-hearted when she voted against me because I lost one of my fondest hopes. That was the only sorority I cared about, and I had my heart set on this one alone.

You won't forget the hate I had for Jean because you and I discussed it several times together. But I never could put it away. I would lie in bed at night and think of ways to get even. Well, last week the chance came.

My manager buzzed me and said she had a promising prospect for that buyer's opening at the D Company. I handle their account. It's the smart place, good pay, nice benefits, and you meet the cream of society.

Can you imagine my feeling when I saw who it was? There she stood: JEAN! She looked at me, I looked at her, and we both knew what the other was thinking.

Since it takes three days to process an interview like this, I took her application. Then I told her to report back, but I knew she wouldn't. She knew it too.

That night I went home, and you know what I was thinking. At last my chance had come. Mother used to say,

"Chickens come home to roost!" Now it was my turn.

But I couldn't sleep. At times like this I keep remembering things from our prayer group. Especially that series we had on "Words from the Cross" made a deep impression on me. What kept coming back to me now were these words, "Father, forgive them, for they know not what they do!"

Well, I battled it for a long time. This was too good to pass up. Yet every time I thought what she had done to me and what I could do to her those words kept coming on strong. So at last I got down on my knees and asked the Lord what I should do. I remember so clearly how we learned that it's no good to pray, "Show me what to do!" without adding "And I will do it!"

Well, you can guess what happened. The next morning I phoned Jean and asked her to come in. I told her the whole story and she got the message. I won't try to describe it except to say it was one of the most beautiful experiences of my whole life. I cried and she cried and we hugged each other.

So, Jean is working for the D Company. We had lunch today. I'm surprised how nice she really is.

Ever since this happened I've had the warmest glow. I feel like I never knew what happiness means until now. Everything else is going great too. I thought you might like to know about this.

Love,
Shirley

It's a fact, isn't it?
If we hate
even one person in the world,
we cannot love any person
with a perfect love.
God put us together that way.

FOUR

"Everybody Is a Little Bit Mental"

Judge not, that you be not judged. For with the judgment you pronounce you will be judged, and the measure you give will be the measure you get.

MATTHEW 7:1-2

Be humble and gentle.
Be patient with each other,
making allowance for each other's faults
because of your love.

EPHESIANS 4:2, TLB

"**E**verybody in the human race is a little bit mental."

This was Grandma Smith's opinion of all the people in all the world. And that's a right broad statement, isn't it? But when Grandma Smith talked I listened. Always. She was only one little old lady, but her ideas packed a wallop for me.

From kindergarten through graduate school I've had some brilliant teachers. But I thank God, too, for my plain-vanilla mentors like Grandma Smith.

This saintly old woman was raised on the prairie, and her education ended with fourth grade. But, like her Good Book puts it, "She opened her mouth with wisdom."

One of her pet subjects was what she called "people peculiarities." The odd. The different. The irregulars. "We gotta love these too," she would say. "If we cross them off our list because they ain't like us, we could end up right lonely."

Grandma Smith never heard the term "tolerance quotient." But she lived it. One more example for Charlie. And is there any one of us who couldn't use a bit more "tolerance quotient"?

As husbands and wives we need it. Every one of us comes into wedlock a bit enamored of our ideal image. But woe unto us if we do not learn that "give a little, take a little" is an absolute must.

And is there a caring parent anywhere who doesn't pray: "Lord, every day, sometimes minute by minute, think through me. For my children's sake, touch my tolerance quotient with your wisdom."

The same thing goes for life outside the home. Here again Grandma Smith is right on, isn't she? Fellow workers, schoolmates, store clerks, kinfolk, the boy delivering our papers, friends, strangers—"Everyone of us is a little bit mental."

Each and every one of us? Yes, that's what she said. But always, without exception, before we ended these discussions she would add: "Now here's something else. With the folks that are *real* mental we got to remember another thing. If we had been through what they been through, we'd be real mental too."

Some very special lady, Grandma Smith. Everybody loved her, including our family. Fact is, we often discussed her sayings around our dinner table. And I will never forget the night one of the younger voices at our table announced:

"You know what I found in our school library today? The title was *Watch Out for the Cooky Inside.* Only they didn't mean cookies. They were talking about mental people like Grandma Smith talks about. Only they said, 'Everybody is a little bit funny.'

"I thought it was neat. And the lady said I could check the book out for you. Want me to?"

> *Our Savior Jesus Christ... gave himself for us, that he might redeem us from all iniquity, and purify unto himself a peculiar people, zealous of good works.* TITUS 2:13-14, KJV

FIVE

On Wedding Bells
and Wedded Bliss

*And so, as those who have been chosen of God, holy
and beloved, put on a heart of compassion, kindness,
humility, gentleness and patience; bearing with one
another, and forgiving each other, whoever has a
complaint against anyone; just as the Lord forgave
you, so also should you. And beyond all these things
put on love, which is the perfect bond of unity.*

COLOSSIANS 3:12-14, NASB

Let us go on unto perfection.

HEBREWS 6:1, KJV

Whatat would you think if you attended a wedding and heard the minister say something like this?

"My dear Harold and Elizabeth, before we proceed to the moment for which we are assembled, I have a word for just you two.

"Harold, you are indeed one handsome groom. As I watched you standing there, I was thinking: Some rental tuxedos don't do much for a man. But yours actually is not half bad.

"And, Elizabeth, when have I seen a bride so lovely? As I saw you coming down the aisle, I was thinking, 'What a fortunate girl to have a mother with taste and a father with adequate credit.'

"The purpose for which we have gathered is to unite you two in holy wedlock. This is a very good thing. So good, in fact, that it stirs feelings scarcely stirred at any other time. By this ceremony we will bring tears to the eyes of your aunts and grandmothers. We will also bring words of considerable scope to the minds of your guests. And I trust, to you.

"For example, at the reception to follow, someone floundering for something to say will settle for this little gem: 'Wasn't it a perfectly beautiful wedding?' To which guest number two, also floundering, will reply, 'Oh, yes. They seem so perfect for each other.'

"Now, right here, Harold and Elizabeth, I adjure you, keep your cool. If all these words about 'perfect' and 'perfectly' should fall on your ears, do not be carried away.

"You better believe me, dear children of the Lord, THIS MAY BE A PERFECTLY BEAUTIFUL WEDDING, BUT THERE ARE NO PERFECT MARRIAGES made at the wedding ceremony.

"Now turning to Scripture, we note these six words straight from Scripture:

Let us go on unto perfection!

"Come to think of it, wouldn't this be an excellent motto to hang in every American home? The mounting divorce rate in our land; the steady parade to a counselor's office; the homes where men and women are sticking it out in a cold war; aren't these all witness to the need for patience and long-range loving?

"But do not despair, Harold and Elizabeth. Yours might become a perfect marriage if you love each other enough for long enough. So when the honeymoon is over and the strains of the organ have been lost from your ears, you better dig in. Love at the maximum requires hard work and steady devotion to duty. It takes patience, long-suffering, tenderness, hurt, sweat, plus biting your lip to shut yourself up at certain moments.

"So there it is, Harold and Elizabeth—you might one day have a perfect love. But it is never lucked into, like bingo. The Lord has ordained that happy marriages must be earned.

"Before we proceed further we will now repeat together (all of us), the chosen text for this service (three times):

Let us go on unto perfection.
Let us go on unto perfection.
Let us go on unto perfection.

HEBREWS 6:1

SIX

"It's His Problem!"

❧

*Love is patient, love is kind. It does not
envy, it does not boast, it is not proud.
It is not rude, it is not self-seeking, it is
not easily angered, it keeps no record of
wrongs.*

1 CORINTHIANS 13:4-5, NIV

*Let the peace of Christ
rule in your hearts.*

COLOSSIANS 3:15

Two psychiatrists officed in the same building. One was on the twenty-third floor. We'll call him "Twenty-Three". The second officed on floor seventeen. "Seventeen" will do for him.

"Twenty-Three" had it made. He really knew how to communicate and his clients came from everywhere. Perhaps what they liked was sinking down in his soft white carpet. Or was it the comfort of those high upholstered chairs in his waiting room?

"Seventeen" had some problems. Problem one was his lack of patients. Problem two was that he drove a plain-vanilla car. So, why would that be a negative? The reason was that his assigned parking spot was next to Twenty-Three's, and Twenty-Three drove a white Cadillac.

Then there was another problem. They came to work at identical times, and they took the same elevator up.

🌺

Now comes the story: With all these downers eating away at him, Seventeen finally blew his cool. One fateful day as they rode upward, he *spit* on Twenty-Three.

But, lo, the victim said not one word. He merely brushed off his coat. Said nothing. Did nothing.

Next day, same thing! Spit again.

Again Twenty-Three kept his cool. Comment: zero.

You can be sure this failure to get through was exasperating Seventeen. Alas, on the third day, he put his full negative into action. This time he spit *all over* "the enemy."

Same song. Next verse. Once more, Twenty-Three took out his kerchief, carefully cleaned himself, said nothing.

You can imagine this was much too much for the lady elevator operator. This time as Seventeen got off at his floor, she closed the door and literally shouted at Twenty-Three, "Sir, didn't you see that man spit on you?"

"Yes," he answered, "I saw it."

"But," she exclaimed, "yesterday he spit on you, too!"

"Come to think of it, you're right."

"And the day before that, sir. He spit on you then."

"Yes. Yes. I do recall."

"Well," she screamed, "aren't you going to do something about it?"

"No." replied the good doctor. "Why should I? *It's his problem!*"

I used that story in a sermon one Sunday. You must understand that in my denomination the world "spit" is a bit uncouth. (Of course, the Bible discusses "spittle" and other embarrassing items with perfect candor.) But still, these days it is wise for preachers to be aware of their clientele.

So as a clergyman, I do know better. Yet some Sundays I can't seem to help myself. Ludicrous wins over decorum.

But this one time I was glad I'd risked it. What made me glad was a letter I received that week from one sweet young housewife.

> *Thank you. Thank you. Thank you. Your very silly story has blessed me to no end. Now when my ugly mother-in-law calls, I have a new handle. At least twice each week she calls, and now because of your story it's so much easier to endure. What I do now is to sit there drinking coffee; reading the paper; the phone hanging from my ear; smiling and repeating silently—*
>
> *Seventeen. Twenty-Three.*
> *Seventeen. Twenty-Three.*

Seventeen. Twenty-Three.

You'd simply never believe how that's blessed me. And here's the bonus—without me to talk back, my mother-in-law soon hangs up. So, once more, thank you, thank you, thank you.

Then, being a devout young woman, she asked me to put her on my prayer list. And particularly, would I pray that this little ritual might eventually develop into a genuine sympathy. Extra nice, don't you think?

And now, over to you for your prayer. But if you really don't need a prayer right now, send one up for me. I seem never to get enough prayers for my own personality quirks. Thank you.

SEVEN

Egyptian Beauty Spots

Do not let your beauty be that of outward adorning, of arranging the hair, of wearing gold, or of putting on of fine apparel; but let it be the hidden person of the heart.

1 PETER 3:3-4

Behold, thou art fair, my love
Behold thou art fair....
Thy lips are like a strand of scarlet
And thy mouth is lovely.

SONG OF SOLOMON 4:1-3, KJV

Would you believe? They were selling "false birthmarks," "artificial moles," and "counterfeit flaws." No fooling.

The place was named "Salon of Enchantment." This was a fashionable neighborhood in one of America's major cities. Here in the window they had a display featuring "Egyptian Beauty Spots." Seems the long ago girls from Sphinxland knew a thing or two about allure. For centuries they've known it.

"And now, girls, we can share it with you."

But that was only one of the signs in their window... all expertly done, tactfully worded. Super chic.

"Contrast—the secret of charm!"

"You can be made-over beautiful!"

"Let perfection bless your loveliness!"

"For lips too big, we have exactly what you need."

"Embellishments for your negatives."

Standing here before their window, my amazed thinker said out loud, "You've got to be kidding." But they weren't. I know because of what I did next. Next I took my amazement to my beautiful wife, and can you believe what she said?

Looking at me with abject pity, she began, "Darling, where have you been? How could you be so innocent? All these years we've been adorning ourselves for your come-on. And you didn't know?"

Fact! I did not know. But ever since that day at the window, I sometimes ponder this whole matter theologically. And here are some questions I come up with:

How much artificiality is OK with the Lord? He made us. Yet

wouldn't he want us to use our judgment for improving our looks all we can? Of course he would.

Have fun, then, fixing yourself up whatever way you think your Creator would approve. But along with your fixing, don't forget this: Imperfections can be assets too. And sometimes even the defects may be just what we need to show off our original charm.

> *So thank you, Lord, for all you gave us to start with. And thank you, too, for the many helps our world offers. Plus thank you for the freedom to use our own judgment. But please, Lord, more than anything, help us to know what looks just right to you. Amen.*

EIGHT

Love Means We Must Sometimes Say, "I'm Sorry"

🌿

Everyone who exalts himself will be humbled, and he who humbles himself will be exalted.
LUKE 14:11

So if you are standing before the altar in the Temple, offering a sacrifice to God, and suddenly remember that a friend has something against you, leave your sacrifice there beside the altar and go and apologize and be reconciled to him....

MATTHEW 5:23-24, TLB

This is about a high school senior. One day he was taken to the superintendent's office for certain observations.

The senior had done well by some measurements. He was student body president; of considerable value to the football team; lead actor in the senior class play. But now, the authorities told "Big Time" he was overdoing the big time.

So here he sat, a special guest in the "super's" confines. And, wouldn't you know, this particular superintendent was a master at bringing down the mighty from their seats. Guiding his prey to a corner now (where he couldn't escape), the superintendent began the meeting.

"Are you aware the faculty right now is up to here with your arrogance? And do you also know your fellow students can hardly stand you?" Etcetera, etcetera, ad infinitum.

It was one thorough job of abasement. And of course the student-body president/football star/lead actor was furious. He didn't have to put up with this from anyone. No way. He would not take it. He stormed out of the man's office. He'd show them.

The next day he stayed away from school. Instead he went down to his favorite spot on the river. Let them come beg him to be in the play. Or maybe the football coach would intercede.

Hour after hour he lay on the mossy riverbank. Hour after hour he looked at the open sky and watched the flowing river. Ah, peace like a river. It soothed his troubled heart and, sure enough, his anger began to subside. Really, wouldn't they be needing him for the big game? Plus, if he stayed away too long might he lose his part in the play?

Naturally this kind of thinking led him to another possibility. Suppose some of these awful things were true, even a little? Had he been too proud of himself? Was he really overbearing? Did he swagger like the man said?

So back to school he went. Humbly. So humbly, in fact, everyone noticed immediately. He was a changed young man. More determined than ever to help his school, to be more considerate, likeable again.

Today, the senior grown to manhood looks back and smiles. Yes, this session in the "super's" office was one of the great moments in his education. It taught him an ultra-valuable lesson. The lesson? When you are criticized, the first place to go is down the hall to a mirror.

This story is no fable. It actually happened just as the facts have been given. And do I need to tell you how I know it's true?

The Old Testament says:
"Before honor is humility" (Proverbs 15:33, KJV).

And the New Testament echoes:
"Humble yourselves in the sight of the Lord,
And he shall lift you up" (James 4:10, KJV).

NINE

"C. Y. K."

❧

Be imitators of God, therefore, as beloved children. And walk in love, as Christ loved us and gave himself up for us....
EPHESIANS 5:1, NIV

Husbands, love your wives.

EPHESIANS 5:25

Much to my surprise, Mr. Carpenter was talking on the phone when I arrived. My eighty-year-old friend had taken a nasty fall, so here he was in the hospital. Yes, here he was, gritting his gums and carefully explaining how they set his broken hip.

He didn't need to tell me who he was talking to. I knew his wife was bedfast at home.

So he motioned me to be seated as though he might be some time on the phone. Then when he began repeating himself he signed off with his familiar three-word good-bye: "C. Y. K." That's all, "C. Y. K."

Hanging up, he apologized for keeping me. "That was the Mrs.," he explained. "Poor girl. She's laid up right now and she's awful worried about me. That's sort of why I got personal so I hope you'll excuse me. You know how they love that carryin' on."

This was so like Mr. Carpenter. He was one of those gritty folks who could never be hurting too much for a little fun. So I rose to his bait. "Tell me, good friend, whatever does your 'C. Y. K.' mean?"

"Oh, that," he chuckled, "that's just a little thing we've had between us more'n fifty years. We only use it when somebody's around and we can't get too personal. What it means is, 'Consider Yourself Kissed!'"

Being a minister, I'm in on numerous marriages. And some of them worry me, especially the men. They worry me when they say, "I don't go for all that sweet talk." Or this, "I wasn't raised that way." Plus the number one downer, "How silly can you get?"

Well listen to me, fellows. If you're at all like that you tune in right here, right now. No woman ever got enough of the warm and tender. That's how God made women.

Take it from an old veteran. You give them all the warmth and tenderness you can dream up today. Then they go to bed and it's all gone away by morning. So what do you do? You start over. Every day you begin again, and really, isn't that rather nice?

Want a Bible verse to write on your heart for a reminder? Proverbs 15:23 (KJV) says,

A word spoken in due season, how good is it.

And there isn't a woman alive who wouldn't agree—"due season" is every day, often.

TEN

"And Hear the Angels Sing"

*Some people have entertained angels
without knowing it.*
HEBREWS 13:2, NIV

The angel of the Lord encamps around those who fear him, and delivers them.

PSALMS 34:7

"Down with the commercial Christmas." Every year at Yule season we hear it again. But is the commercial Christmas altogether negative?

I know one year when it wasn't for one couple.

In an effort to save their marriage they had been coming for consultation. We'd done the best we could, but now they'd decided to call it quits. Yet both being considerate of other people's feelings, they'd determined to wait until after the holidays. For their children's sake especially, they would postpone their breakup.

Naturally they had some Christmas shopping to do. So, since they were on speaking terms they'd do that together too.

Now comes the miracle.

One day they stopped in a downtown bank. Was it a coincidence that every year this particular bank sponsored their own Christmas choir? Employees and customers joined to praise the Lord for another Christmas together. For many years they'd been doing this. And now came my couple to cash a check.

Straight from them, the story.

"Do you believe in miracles? What happened to us was sure like a miracle. As we stood there listening, all of a sudden we both felt something. We looked at each other and knew we ought to try it again. Maybe we could make it after all."

Of course I asked the question you would ask, "What was the choir singing?"

"Well," he replied, "we don't remember all the words but we sure caught this one line. Fact is, we decided to make it our theme song. Have you ever heard it?

Oh rest beside the weary road and hear the angels sing.

"Well, we both agreed this was one of the most beautiful things we'd ever heard. And do you know what else? Before we even realized it, we were holding hands. I mean for the first time in months we were holding hands. Like I say, the whole thing was pure miracle."

What a story. One broken marriage. One traditional bank-sponsored Christmas choir. One familiar old carol with exactly the right words at exactly the right time.

So now every Christmas I can drive through the decorated streets; past all the lovely homes with twinkling lights; shop downtown with all its Yuletide bid for business; all these I can do with enthusiasm. And my mind has taken a turn here. Now it seems clear to me that the Lord can reach his own any way he wishes.

But why should I be surprised? Doesn't the Good Book say he can use even the wrath of men to praise him? Of course he would have no problem reaching his own through a bank-sponsored choir. He can use whatever he wants, whenever he wants, and wherever.

Yes, yes, yes. At Christmas and all year long in church or any-where, any time it's a great song, isn't it?

Oh, rest beside the weary road
And hear the angels sing.

ELEVEN

Soul Clutter

*Lay not up for yourselves treasures upon earth,
where moth and rust doth corrupt, and where
thieves break through and steal: But lay up for
yourselves treasures in heaven, where neither
moth nor rust doth corrupt, and where thieves
do not break through and steal. For where your
treasure is, there will your heart be also.*

MATTHEW 6:19-21, KJV

*F*inally, brethren, whatsoever things are true,
whatsoever things are honest,
whatsoever things are just,
whatsoever things are pure,
whatsoever things are lovely,
whatsoever things are of good report;
if there be any virtue, and if there be any praise,
think on these things.

PHILIPPIANS 4:8, KJV

The Lord thought up a good thing when he made us all so different, didn't he? And here's one of my all-time favorites, from a New York newspaper. They called him a "recluse." It was long ago I read of him. But his lifestyle made me think and think and think. About me.

"Recluse" lived in a once-fashionable townhouse. Obviously fine furnishings, originally. But here, there, and everywhere were boxes, boxes, boxes. Every one of them containing string, every one of them labeled. Plus he had stashed away string in sacks, jars, bags, drawers, cupboards. String, string, string he'd found on the streets and who knows where all. String tenderly saved and all carefully docketed.

"String two feet long," "String fourteen-and-one-half inches," "String two inches," etc., etc., etc. But what fascinated the reporter most was a box marked:

String too short to save

Fascinating, isn't it? Worth a laugh for sure. But is that all? No. Some lessons never go away and even today when I think of this unusual gentleman I find myself asking: "Who am I to point the finger? Is my life over-done with clutter? Do I tend too much toward keeping what stuff and junk I should let go?"

❧

In addition to all kinds of personal questions, the string recluse did another thing for me. He led me to activate a promise I'd made to myself. For five years, on the way to and from my car I'd seen that sign, "Church Storeroom."

"Some day," I vowed, "as the pastor here, I must research the church storeroom. Yes. I will dedicate an entire day to the possibilities herein."

Understand this was one huge storeroom; at least six times the size of your garage. Understand also, this was really no sacrificial commitment on my part. In all honesty I love junk. I love scrounging around. I love the unknown.

So into the unknown I went, and I share with you now my findings.

🌿

Contents: (a) One bust of George Washington done in plaster and used in a February play. Date: 1917. Somebody had thought it valuable. Save it. (b) Scenery. Huge sections of scenery used in "The Willing Workers" chorale of 1929. "Mustn't discard this. Could come in handy some day." (c) World maps. Stacks of them. Purchased for an annual Mission Training School and still stored in the shipper's box. Date: 1909. Indeed, spare these maps. (d) Twenty-volume set of big, big books. Labeled "History of the Boer Wars." Donated by one Widow Wilson when she moved to a nursing home. Intended for the church library. Dedicated to the fond memory of her late husband. (Wonder what she really thought of him?) (e) Things too numerous to mention (or are they?): pictures, vases, lamps, an elk's head, old clothes, flower baskets, costumes, manger sets, and of all things—some girlie magazines!

Let's dedicate a moment to that last item. Don't you wonder? Had some guilt-stricken soul decided to swear off his "hobby"? Or was it that he simply couldn't part with his treasures? And where could a safer place be found? Ah, yes. The church storeroom!

Yet, like I said, who am I to sit in judgment? Don't we all tend to overstuff our minds with things we should have let go?

The Bible makes it plain that "cleansing," "purging," "new life" are of ultra importance. And doesn't the Lord also promise this? He himself will purify the inner me if I ask him.

Maybe now is just the time to ask him.

Heavenly Father, you know what I should keep and what I should cast away. Help me to unclutter my personal little oddities. Even the ones like "string too short to save." Amen.

TWELVE

Ten Rules to
Simplify Your Living

꒰❀꒱

*Do not be anxious about your life, what you
shall eat or what you shall drink, nor about
your body, what you shall put on. Is not life
more than food, and the body more than
clothing? Look at the birds of the air: they
neither sow nor reap nor gather into barns,
and yet your heavenly Father feeds them. Are
you not of more value than they?*

Matthew 6:25-26

Humble yourselves therefore under the mighty hand of God, that he may exalt you in due time. Casting all your care upon him; for he careth for you.

1 PETER 5:6-7, KJV

Simplify? Why simplify?

These "Ten Rules to Simplify Your Living" were written fifty years ago. Martha and I were under tremendous pressure at that time in our lives, and we needed these rules very, very much. I was pastor of a mammoth church, with countless demands on my time and energy, plus more and more demands on my love. Martha was my prayer partner and daily companion. Together we studied the Bible. Together we asked God to show us how to manage the work he had given us to do.

Each day we would pray together, then ask ourselves, "What would God say about...?" Eventually we came up with this list that helped us to keep the most important things at the top of the list—and to let things go that weren't that important. Together we discovered that

If we will let him, our Lord will live in us
and love through us.

No doubt you have times when you are frustrated and much too busy. I hope these simple rules will help you to live a more serene life in your harried world. Or better still, ask the Lord to give you his rules for you!

1 MAKE SURE YOU NEED TO SIMPLIFY YOUR LIVING. Your problem could be one of inertia. Your life may seem heavy and complex because you aren't doing enough. Selfishness never simplifies—it complicates.

2 REMEMBER WHY YOU ARE LIVING. Put the will of God first in your activity. You unclutter your life when you have one pivotal purpose on which your living swings.

3 DROP YOUR USELESS GOALS. You may be wearing yourself out on things that do not matter. You frustrate yourself when you dedicate your life to the unimportant.

4 DON'T TRY TO DO IT ALL YOURSELF. If God had wanted you to be six people, he would have divided you up. Leave some of the world's building to others.

5 USE YOUR SUBCONSCIOUS AS AN UNSEEN HELPER. Move some of your living over into good habits which you repeat until they become second nature.

6 LIVE ONE DAY AT A TIME. You can plan for tomorrow and hope for the future—but don't live there. Live this day well and tomorrow's strength will come tomorrow.

7 ENJOY WHAT YOU'RE DOING WHILE YOU'RE DOING IT. Don't allow yourself to think that happiness comes at five o'clock, or at the evening's party, or when you finally fall asleep. Learn to live in the present moment.

8 DEVELOP A HOBBY. A regular change of activity will keep you fresh. Time spent at play is time well spent.

9 IF IT IS IMPOSSIBLE TO SLOW YOUR WORLD DOWN, SLOW YOURSELF DOWN. Learn to shift into overdrive. When you can't alter the whirling pace, retire to your inner sanctuary and alter yourself.

10 ADOPT THE PERFECT PATTERN, WHICH IS CHRIST. Study this humble carpenter of Galilee whose life cut history squarely in two. Follow him as he lives a mighty life in quiet confidence. "Let this mind be in you" (Philippians 2:5, KJV).

THIRTEEN

The Night I Learned about God's Forgiveness

But when he was yet a great way off, his father saw him and had compassion, and ran, and fell on his neck, and kissed him.
LUKE 15:20, KJV

*F*athers, *provoke not your children to anger,*
lest they be discouraged.

Most boys cause some trouble, and I was no exception. One year my buddies and I enrolled together for a junior high church conference. Which was too bad for the conference, but it was sure to be fun for us. There may have been six others like us somewhere, but let's hope not.

On the first night we sneaked out for an escapade. We began by raiding the kitchen edibles. Next we squirted a hose in the girls' cabin window. That done, we pushed a farm wagon up the chapel aisle. Then we set some alarm clocks to go off in assembly next morning. Finally, off to town for the midnight show.

At last, back we went to the conference grounds. Tired, but oh so pleased with ourselves, we removed our shoes and slipped quietly up the steps of our dormitory.

Will I ever forget the next three minutes? No. Halfway up the steps, suddenly a voice from below said, "Stop right where you are."

We did.

Then the voice, which we recognized as the dean's, went on:

"I don't know who you are and I don't want to know. But this is a religious conference, and I'm going to ask you to bow your heads while I pray."

Then came one of the most beautiful prayers I've ever heard. I do so wish it might have been recorded for posterity. Recalling them now, the words went something like this:

Dear Lord, up here on the steps are some boys who aren't where they ought to be. You know them all by name and they are your boys. Forgive them for breaking the rules of our camp and love them anyway. In the years to come help them to remember this night and protect them from serious trouble elsewhere. Now see them to bed tonight and every night of their lives. And please make them more like Jesus who kept the rules and still lived a good life.... Amen.

You think that's beautiful? It is. But hear now the benediction. After the Amen, the voice said:

"Boys, I have a flashlight in my hand. I will count to ten and then turn it on. Goodnight."

As I look back now, I am absolutely sure of this: that moment was one of the major influences which led me to the ministry.

That night I got a new idea of God. I had never known him like this. But that's how he is. The Lord of the Universe isn't so concerned with where we've been. He only wants to know where we are now. "What have you been doing?" is not his major question. "What will you do in the future?"—that's what counts most with him.

STRAIGHT FROM THE LORD—

*Two words for one sure way to let
people know they are really loved:*

Forgiveness and Mercy

Recommended Reading Often
LUKE 15:11-32

FOURTEEN

Facing the Truth about Me

🌿

*Each of you must put off falsehood and speak
truthfully to his neighbor, for we are all members
of one body…. Do not let any unwholesome talk
come out of your mouths, but only what is help-
ful for building others up according to their needs,
that it may benefit those who listen.*
EPHESIANS 4:25, 29, NIV

*Sometimes a good way
to let people know we really love them
is to thank them
when they have had the courage
to help us improve ourselves.*

*Don't kick if I kick. I never waste my time cutting bad specks
out of rotten apples. Whenever I criticize, you can know I still
think you are worth developing.*

Signed: The Boss

My new bride and I were sitting in the reception room of
a large Chicago printing firm. In huge block letters the
above message from Mr. Big was hanging behind glass
in a prominent spot.

"You like that?" she asked.

"Sure do," I replied. "Says a lot, doesn't it? Copy it down, will
you? Might come in handy."

So she copied it down, and on the way home she read it aloud
to me again. We discussed it between endearments. (This was the
week following our honeymoon.) Then she made me a deal.

"You know who my favorite preacher is, don't you?" she
asked. Since this was Monday morning after a perfectly horrible
sermon, I had that feeling: "Something's coming!" And it was.

Picking her way carefully, she began to recite all the things she
liked about her pet pulpiteer. But before she finished, she added,
"Tell you what! Let's have an agreement. I'll help you be even a
better preacher if you'll help me some places where I need
improvement."

Then with her softest touch, she went on, "There are some
things you do, darling, that bother me. I'm sure you don't even
know you're doing them. But if they bother me a little, I wonder,
might they be an awful bother to people who don't know all the
wonderful things I know about you? Would you like me to help
you?" (Some women are such experts in delicate relationships,
aren't they? Like putting together propositions which couldn't
possibly be rejected by any man in his right mind.) So we made a
compact. And from those early days in my student church to forever after, she was my super tutor.

I give you now some examples:

"Sweetheart, today I counted sixteen places you said *'dee*scover.' It's *'dis*cover.' Get it?"

I got it. Next:

"Sometimes, while you're preaching, you put your hand over your lips. When you do this, it sounds like you have marbles in your mouth."

I got that one too.

"Lately you've started taking your glasses off and twirling them in your hand. It's terribly distracting. See what I mean? (Twirling her glasses.) I don't want to miss any of the good things you're saying."

"You keep saying, 'Don't miss this point.' That's an insult, sweetheart. Sounds like you're afraid I haven't been listening. And, honestly, I listen all the time."

Enough? No. No. No.

"Do you realize that you always shout when you're not sure of yourself?"

Not until she told me, I didn't.

"*Extrapolate* is a fun word to say, but it's not right for the pulpit. How many people actually know what extrapolate means? Not many. And remember what you yourself always say, 'Why irritate people if you don't need to?'"

Time to call this off? Not quite.

"Don't pull your ear like this, (pulling her ear) when you're preaching. You do have nice ears, but...."

And finally:

"Honey, why do you constantly rattle your coins in your pocket when you're about to make a point? The deacons must already know we need a raise."

End of list. At least for right now.

You understand these were not all given me at the same sitting. "Sitting?" Yes, "sitting." As I recall, most of these suggestions were presented while we were cozied up on our rocking love seat. Wonder why?

But you don't wonder about this, do you? It's a fortunate man who has one friend loving enough to know the negatives, and share them.

The psalmist tells us that our Lord

> *"Desirest truth in the inward parts."* PSALMS 51:6, KJV

And the writer of Ephesians says,

> *"Speaking the truth in love,*
> *we are to grow up in every way."* EPHESIANS 4:15

Could there ever be
a finer way
to let people know
we really love them
than by living
these two verses together?

FIFTEEN

Ten Rules for
Managing Criticism

✺

*If when you do right and suffer for it you take
it patiently, you have God's approval. For to
this you have been called, because Christ also
suffered for you, leaving you an example, that
you should follow in his steps.*
1 PETER 2:20-21

The words of the wicked lie in wait for blood,
but the mouth of the upright delivers men.

PROVERBS 12:6

1 CRITICISM IS OFTEN A COMPLIMENT. The many barbs in daily flight only strike those who raise their heads above ground level.

2 BE HONEST WITH YOURSELF. Accept the fact that in you there may be faults which are open to censure. If you keep humble, criticism need not jar you.

3 INVITE CRITICISM FROM YOUR FRIENDS. If you do this, when it comes from your enemies you will be broken in. Practice makes perfect.

4 EVEN THE BITTEREST CRITICISM CAN MAKE YOU BETTER IF YOU WILL LET IT. When you burn with anger you may destroy the passport to your own improvement.

5 SOME CRITICISM SHOULD BE IGNORED. This is especially true if it is prompted by false motives. Don't let unhappy people hold the key to your happiness.

6 KEEP THE CRITICISM IN ITS RIGHT PROPORTION. Everybody hasn't heard. Lots of people don't care. One bad word doesn't cancel out what good there is in you.

7 LET CRITICISM MAKE YOU MORE KINDLY. When you are criticized, remind yourself that you have criticized too. Is this criticism a boomerang which started in your own heart?

8 PRAY FOR YOUR CRITIC. It will not only improve him, it will neutralize your bitterness. Allowed to flow freely, hate can destroy your health and steal your happiness.

9 CHECK THIS CRITICISM AGAINST THE MASTER CRITIC. What does God tell you? Away at the center of your soul, how does it look there?

10 WHEN YOU HAVE CHECKED TO BE SURE YOU ARE RIGHT, GO AHEAD. In quiet confidence finish the thing you have started. The promises of God are to those who endure.

NOTE: These "Ten Rules for Managing Criticism" were produced by Martha and me, just as we compiled the "Ten Rules for Conquering Worry" (chapter 20). Nothing has changed since we penned these rules so many years ago. Human needs are still the same.

SIXTEEN

The Boomerang of Envy

❦

*Let us have no self-conceit, no provoking of
one another, no envy of one another.*
GALATIANS 5:26

*Y*ou shall not set your desire on your neighbor's house
or land,... or anything that belongs to your neighbor.

DEUTERONOMY 5:21, NIV

At one time in our young married life, Martha and I raised collie dogs. Our kennel name was Hallelujah, and Hallelujah collies did very well. So well that we attended numerous dog shows, and here we discovered something. What we discovered was that collie people are even more interesting than their dogs. And one of these was Ernest, a Minnesota farmer.

Along with his collies, Ernest raised Manx cats, Guernsey cows, and Belgian horses. Since I'd always had a yen for farming we became extra good friends. And yes, I envied him.

We saw each other very little but corresponded often. And in one of my letters I confessed my envy. What could be finer than to live on a farm in Minnesota? A beautiful dairy herd. Horses. Chickens for eggs, pigs for pork, sweet corn on the table, what a life. Plus what a place to raise the family. Ah, Ernest, sometimes I wish you were here and I was there.

What happened next? You may have guessed, but I'd never given thought one to the things he described. This was panic time on his farm. The snow was eleven feet high. He was down to his last hay. The animals were all suffering. Some of them, he was afraid, might not come through. Milk production had fallen to near zero; water pipes were frozen; phones were out of order; schools were closed; the children were getting on each other's nerves. In short, if it didn't thaw soon, he was afraid they would all be ready for the funny farm.

Then he added this winsome note:

"Interesting that you should be envying me! That's exactly how I've been feeling about you. My father was an Episcopal rector, and I have always had a suppressed desire to follow in his footsteps. So I've been thinking about you with your lovely new church. People to hear you preach. Men, women, boys, girls to influence. An organization to run. The sick and sorrowing to visit. Folks to help. Yes, I envy you!"

Then, to top it off, he sent me this anonymous poem:

> How perfectly wonderful things would be
> If we could get back to simplicity.
> A scenic and picturesque piece of land
> With all of our livelihood right at hand.
>
> No bills every month for our water and heat.
> We'd grow all our vegetables, fruit, and our meat.
> The income we'd need would, of course, be so small
> That taxes would almost be nothing at all.
>
> The crops might not grow and the pigs might all die,
> The wood might run out and the well might go dry;
> We might not have money for clothes and all that,
> But ain't farm life grand — from my steam-heated flat?

Questions for musing: Am I getting the most out of my life here where I am? Do I spend too much time thinking how nice it would be elsewhere? And do I miss a host of good things all about me because my thoughts are too much "over there"?

Wonder if thoughts like these are what the Bible means when it says:

> *This is the day which the Lord has made;*
> *let us rejoice and be glad in it!*
> PSALMS 118:24

SEVENTEEN

"Ninety-Two and Eighty-Eight"

✿

Looking unto Jesus, the author and finisher of our faith;
who for the joy that was set before him endured the cross....
HEBREWS 12:2, KJV

Since you became alive again, so to speak, when Christ arose from the dead, now set your sights on the rich treasures and joys of heaven where he sits beside God in the place of honor and power.

COLOSSIANS 3:1, TLB

Imet one of the loveliest people I ever knew when she was ninety-two. It was a high privilege to visit her, and I always came away feeling much better. Since others felt the same way, she had a host of friends. She loved freely and was freely loved. Her house was filled with flowers and plants. Her walls were covered with homey pictures, and there was a gentle serenity in all she had, all she did, all she said.

A few blocks down the street lived a woman of eighty-eight. The shades were drawn at her house, and there was a sinister air about the place. No sooner did I enter her door than she began to chew on me for not having come more often. "Nobody," she moaned, "ever visits me." She was right—nobody did. The reason was obvious. She was thoroughly negative. Interspersed in whatever she said were snatches of criticism, judgment, gossip. Bitterness flooded from her pent-up heart, and I would go away feeling like eighty-eight myself.

Total contrast! Ninety-two blossomed. Eighty-eight withered. Yet both these women were members of the same church. Each had an admirable record of Sunday school attendance, service in church work, faithfulness at worship. Each had been around a long time. They were pioneers of the same community.

So, what made the difference? Money? No! They both had enough to keep them nicely. Tragedy? No! Each had buried her husband, brothers, sisters, children, friends. Suffering? No! There was very little difference in their physical condition. Still they were opposite as day and night. Why?

One day I had a few minutes after calling on them both, so I scribbled some notes: "What made one a lesson in how to grow old gracefully and the other an example of how not to?"

On my scratch pad today I find these observations:

Ninety-two was thinking of others. She was forever asking about my family and about things at church. "How are those folks that went through the fire?" Was there anything she could do to help? Eighty-eight only whined that nobody cared about her.

Ninety-two was thankful. Overwhelmed by how good life had been to her; how wonderful people were; how grateful she was for her many blessings. Not eighty-eight. Her mood was complain, complain, and, "Oh, isn't it awful?"

So what else made the difference? One answer was that my first friend had the light of optimism in her eye. And where did she get it? I think she got it from *looking to the future with high hope.* Tomorrow, next week, and oh, wouldn't it be wonderful when she got to heaven?

If you'd been her pastor, you'd have done what I did. Every time I was with her, I'd move her toward the heaven theme. And I remember as if it were yesterday some of the things she told me. Over and over I heard them, so I can give them to you word for word.

"Well, to begin with, when we get to heaven we'll never die again. Won't that be wonderful?"...(Did you ever think of that before? I never had.) Then she'd go on, "Imagine what it will mean to see all the people we've said good-bye to. Did you know I had a little girl who died? She was only six weeks old, and I can hardly wait to see her. For a long time I fussed on whether she'd be grown up now or still a baby. And guess what settled me down? I asked the Lord, and he told me in heaven she can be either one. Sometimes I can rock her like I never got to. Then sometimes we can be grown-ups together. Did you ever hear anything more beautiful than that?

"Now here's another thing. You know I don't sing in the choir. I can't even play the piano. I'm just plain not musical. Well, I think they'll let me do something about that in heaven too.

"You want to hear more? All right, this one I wouldn't tell to just anybody, but you're my pastor and I need to talk about it sometimes. When I was young this one person hurt me so bad. Worst thing that ever happened to me. I think heaven will change my feelings about that too. I'll be so glad to be rid of the hurt.

"And oh say, think of all the Bible characters we'll get to meet in heaven, and visit with. Of course I want to see Jesus. I suppose he'll be just like he was in the Bible. Don't you think that will be one of the greatest things ever?"

So on and on she'd go. Then she'd stop herself with: "Now I better quit and you tell me what you think. Not many people you can talk to like this. But isn't it fun?"

So I would share with her, and it *was* fun. Then before our prayer together I said, "Do you know, I think I've discovered something. What you think about heaven must be one of the things that makes you so happy here on earth."

"Oh, I know that's true," she'd say. "And I'll tell you something else: *I think it's easier to really love everybody when you're happy.*"

Now that's worth a retake, isn't it?

*"I think it's easier to really love everybody
when you're happy."*

EIGHTEEN

Homer's Prayer for Divine Measurement

Do not think of yourself more highly than you ought, but rather think of yourself with sober judgment, in accordance with the measure of faith God has given you.

ROMANS 12:3, NIV

By your standard of measure it shall be measured to you; and more shall be given you besides.

MARK 4:24, NASB

Homer has an unusual evening prayer. When the house is quiet and everyone else is in bed, he stills himself in the big chair and waits. Then after he is completely hushed he prays:

> Dear Lord, I want to see myself as you see me. I don't want to see me through my own eyes—I'm prejudiced. I'm not asking to see Homer as his friends see Homer—that could be too good. I don't want to see Homer as his enemies see him, that's too bad. Show me myself *as I look to you!*

Then he lingers in his big chair and closes his eyes. What happens? This is his report:

1. He senses that his life was created for greater purposes than self-satisfaction. As he thinks that through there comes over him a tremendous feeling of worth. THIS GIVES HIM PURPOSE!

2. He sees his faults in true perspective. If he has been deceiving himself, he is brought face to face with the facts. THIS GIVES HIM HONESTY!

3. He has a place to take the criticisms which come his way. The Inner Voice tells him whether he should be bothered by these things or dismiss them as irrelevant. THIS GIVES HIM PEACE.

4. He sees possibilities which excite him. These are good things about himself he may have overlooked. They make him realize how great the future could be. THIS GIVES HIM HOPE!

5. He gets his life back on the right track. As he muses on these things he feels a reorientation of his soul to the Upward Way. THIS GIVES HIM DIRECTION.

Purpose...Honesty...Peace...Hope...Direction!

Homer's prayer *is* one great prayer, isn't it?

Do you wonder that he is one of the truly great men I know? Through his affiliation with a national organization, he gives his time to rebuilding broken lives. Hundreds of men and women in many places have felt the influence of Homer's attunement to the Lord.

The official catechism of many churches begins with:

"What is man's chief end?"

And it answers:

"Man's chief end is to glorify God and enjoy Him forever!"

Wouldn't it be some world if every one of us regularly checked our lives against Homer's prayer for divine measurement?

Thought for letting others know we really love them:

Our Lord has all the love there is. The more we develop ways of staying tuned to him, the more he can love through us. This is the perfect way: His way. "God IS love."

NINETEEN

Words Can Burn Us Up

You aren't made unholy by eating non-kosher food!
It is what you say and think that makes you unclean.
MATTHEW 15:11, TLB

*T*hey sharpen their tongues like swords,
ready their bows for arrows of poison words.
They shoot at the innocent from ambush,
shoot without risk, and catch them unaware.

PSALMS 64:4-5

Wwe have a friend who came up with her third ulcer recently. The doctor was at a loss to diagnose her problem. She lived a reasonably quiet life. She had no major worries, at least not on the surface. She wouldn't impress you at all as unusually nervous.

So the internist sent her to a psychiatrist. Like you maybe, I'm somewhat bewildered by all these inner labels: "ids," "egos," "superegos," and the like.

But her analyst is a winner. He uncovered the trouble immediately. And the way we know is that she's getting better.

※

In rummaging through her childhood, they discovered a forgotten fact about her home. Conversation there slanted heavily to the negatives. Many families, her analyst told her, have this same dangerous tendency: Their meal time talk majors in the awful-awfuls, such as:

"I can't stomach her"—"I'd like to choke her"—"I'm eating my heart out"—"He cooks my goose."

The result, says the wise man, is a slow burn inside.

As our friend searched her background for these echoes, she found numerous possibilities. This is her report: "Many times my mother would come to the table with things like this: 'I'm going to tell you an awful thing I heard today, but first we'll have the blessing.' Now, 'Like I said, I just can't believe Eunice would ever do anything like that, can you?' And on and on. Then with the dessert she would serve up more of her downers, usually ending with: 'I guess we just plain can't trust anybody these days.'"

Then one friend concluded, "I remember it all so well now. All our mealtimes were complete with roast relatives, stewed neighbors, fried teachers, all kinds of ulcer-makers."

You will be glad to know she's doing so much better. Her burning inside is subsiding with a feeling of permanent recovery.

Our Bible says, "The tongue is a fire," and "Behold how great a matter a little fire kindleth" (James 3:5, KJV).

This verse has the feel of the real, doesn't it? Forests have been destroyed from one little match.

Certainly there must be times to share the hard things. Every home should have its hours to unburden.

How? One family I know has set up some safeguards. It's a list of questions for mutual musing:

"Do we keep our ears cocked for negatives and rush to pass them on?"..."Is the conversation at our table bent in the direction of anxiety, anger, and, 'Isn't it awful?'"..."Has our marriage become a sounding board for evil tidings and excessive melancholy?"..."Is the major trend at our house constructive or destructive?"..."Are the words we share burning us up or warming our souls?"

And one more question for some deep-deep think:

What does all this have to do with
letting people know we really love them?

Better is a dry morsel with quiet
than a house full of feasting with strife.
PROVERBS 17:1

TWENTY

Ten Ways to Conquer Worry

❧

Who of you by worrying can add a single hour to his life?... So do not worry, saying, "What shall we eat?" or "What shall we drink?" or "What shall we wear?" For the pagans run after all these things, and your heavenly Father knows that you need them.

MATTHEW 6:27, 31-32, NIV

But seek first his kingdom and his righteousness, and all these things will be given you as well. Therefore do not worry about tomorrow, for tomorrow will worry about itself. Each day has enough trouble of its own.

MATTHEW 6:33-34, NIV

Why are these worry thoughts in a book called *How to Make People Really Feel Loved?* Isn't this the most certain answer: *Worry is a love thief.* So, if perchance you, too, are sometimes harassed and harried, I share with you now my ten prayers for worry concern.

1 "Lord, help me to keep in mind that THERE IS A BIG DIFFERENCE BETWEEN NERVOUS WORRY AND HEALTHY CONCERN.... each day, all day, may I do your work without fussing."

2 "Heavenly Father, may I never forget that a good father puts his child to bed because his child needs rest.... THANK YOU, LORD, FOR MY OWN SLEEP AND QUIET, PLUS TIMES TO DO NOTHING."

3 "O Divine Creator, you made things to grow and things to diminish.... Help me to remember that MY PROBLEMS DO HAVE A WAY OF SHRINKING AS I DRAW CLOSER TO THEM.... Thank you for all those times you actually have reduced my troubles overnight."

4 "Good Lord, keep me away from the land of 'What if.' Help me to remember THERE IS JUST AS MUCH CHANCE IT WON'T HAPPEN AS THAT IT WILL.... Thank you. Thank you."

5 "Creator of the Universe and me, MAY I NEVER FORGET THAT THERE ARE HIDDEN RESERVES IN ALL OF US.... You put them there. You can wake mine in my hours of crisis.... I praise you for the strength you stashed away for my emergencies. How great thou art."

6 "O Divine Mind, give me the wisdom to know that there are SOME THINGS I AM MEANT TO CONTROL BUT SOME ARE NOT FOR ME.... I am truly grateful that you have equipped me with an effective 'worry or not' sorter. Help me to use it well for you."

7 "Lord of the healthy mind, MAKE ME WARY OF JEALOUSY.... May I ever remember that other people only look as if they have no worries.... And please remind me often that I really would not like to trade places with anyone."

8 "KEEP ME CHECKING ON MY GOALS, LORD. OFTEN.... When I am worrying over false ambitions, correct me.... If I am reaching where I shouldn't reach, tap me then too.... And yes, sometimes when I'm getting lazy, guide me to new dreams, new goals for you."

9 "God of all the people in all the world, WHEN I AM UNDULY ANXIOUS, REMIND ME TO STOP AND DO SOMETHING FOR SOMEONE... a shut-in, a troubled friend, some good cause.... Make me one of your everyday missionaries to the everyday needs of others."

10 "Father, Son, and Holy Spirit, MINUTE BY MINUTE, DAY BY DAY, HOUR BY HOUR, HELP ME TO TRUST YOU MORE.... Forever and forever may I love you more, that I may more and more love others for you.

"So may it be—Amen."

TWENTY-ONE

The Miracle of Persistent Love

Is any one of you sick? He should call the elders of the church to pray over him and anoint him with oil in the name of the Lord. And the prayer offered in faith will make the sick person well; the Lord will raise him up.

JAMES 5:14-15, NIV

Ask, and it shall be given you;
seek, and ye shall find;
knock, and it shall be opened unto you.

LUKE 11:9, KJV

This story is true. It is about Emma and George. Emma was a housewife, George a hardware salesman.

Emma was one of those whose very presence draws people together. She was president of our church women the year they reorganized. That took considerable savvy for someone so young. But through it all Emma moved like a queen. She compromised in matters unimportant. She stood her ground in things that counted. And where she felt herself inadequate she asked the Lord to help her, which he did. All of us were so proud of her— pastor, parents, husband. We all admired Emma.

Then suddenly, everything seemed to go wrong for her. She had her first baby, and what should have been a happy time, became a disaster. This was one of those cases where a woman changes personality completely. Scary. Sinister. Finally came the tragic news from her doctors. The only safe place was our state hospital for the mentally ill. In her present condition she might destroy her child. Yes, she might also turn against her husband, her parents, the neighbors, anyone. So they took her away.

Word came back occasionally but no change. Her parents took the baby. Her young husband came to church alone. Then gradually, you know how it goes. Weeks went by and the embers of concern faded away.

But they would not die in George's heart. He was a leader in our church, and he remembered the day this fine young couple joined us. So he went now and then to see the young father. He checked occasionally on the baby, and then he paid a visit to the doctor. Would it be all right for him to stop at the hospital and see Emma? He was a traveling salesman, and his work took him in that direction.

"Yes, yes, of course": a bright green light from the doctor. So George stopped now and then to see her. When she was feeling well enough, they could visit across the separation screen. He could even hold her hand through the opening as he prayed for her.

At first she showed little interest, but George refused to give up. He would tell her about the lilacs in bloom in her front yard. "We've finished the new addition to the church. And, oh yes, your brother is playing on the high school basketball team this year."

Then one day, to everyone's surprise, she asked about the baby and her husband. For just a moment George thought he saw a flicker of her former self.

For several months he continued dropping in now and then. Each time he was sure she showed a bit more interest. Each time he would pray with her and tell her, "Everyone in the church is praying for you. We love you."

Then one day George received a letter saying he wouldn't need to stop any more. This was a letter from Emma, and *she was coming home for Christmas.* The doctor even said if everything went well he'd let her stay. How could she ever tell him what his visits had meant? Would he also please express her thanks to everyone who had been praying for her?

So Emma came home. That year there was something extra special about Christmas. In our church, in the whole town, everywhere. Hardly a dry eye as people heard the good news. *Emma's doctor said she was completely healed and she could stay.*

A true miracle.

What really happened? Was her recovery only a natural event in the passing of time? Could the miraculous cure be attributed to some wise doctor's therapy? Might it have been the work of a new wonder drug? Or could it have been a real Christmas angel? Maybe a host of them, praising God and singing, "Glory to God in the highest"?

The Bible says:

The effectual fervent prayer of a righteous man availeth much.

JAMES 5:16, KJV

And it's a verse for women too, isn't it? How many miracles have been wrought by daughters of the Lord? So isn't it a verse for all of us? Always, prayer is a prelude to letting people know we really love them.

TWENTY-TWO

Fighting Fair

❧

*"In your anger, do not sin": Do not let the sun go
down while you are still angry, and do not give
the devil a foothold.... Get rid of all bitterness,
rage and anger, brawling and slander, along with
every form of malice. Be kind and compassionate
to one another, forgiving each other, just as in
Christ God forgave you.*

EPHESIANS 4:26, 31-32, NIV

For we all stumble in many ways: If anyone does not stumble in what he says, he is a perfect man, able to bridle the whole body.... But no one can tame the tongue; it is a restless evil, and full of deadly poison.

JAMES 3:2, 8, NIV

In the rural area where I grew up there were some unforgettable expressions. You'd have remembered them, too, particularly these sayings for embarrassing moments.

"You put your foot in it."

"Somebody goofed."

"She pulled a loo loo."

You could spell this last one "lu lu" if you prefer. But here's one reserved for the really big boners; and, at this minute, Herby qualified big time. If you don't understand exactly what it means, do have some rural soul explain it for you.

"OUT IN THE BARNYARD, THE JACKASS BRAYED."

Now... here came Herby and his crumbled wife. But wasn't he crumbled too? Indeed he was. He'd allowed himself the luxury of one line too many.

To get the full scenario you'd need to see this little lady. She was somewhat attractive, but not altogether so. Clarice had the largest feminine ears I've ever seen. I mean these were great big ears. Fact is, they were so big they made the rest of her look somewhat incidental.

Of course, Herby knew this. Yet she was very clever at wearing her hair to camouflage the oversize hearing equipment. But on the particular night of their latest battle, there was simply no hiding. In this particular fuss they were having now, her hair went absolutely everywhere.

Suddenly, at the height of battle, he caught sight of her exposed ears. Without thinking how it would hurt, he put hands on hips and began to laugh. This can be a very good technique if it means, "You're so cute when you're mad." But cute was not what Herby had in mind. At top crescendo the jackass brayed: "Those ears of yours! They look like bat wings!"

I will spare you further details. He won that particular conflict as she collapsed in a flood of tears. So chalk up one more battle for his side. Or then again, with some things in marriage don't we lose when we win? So true, and this was one such time.

I am glad to report they are still together. Yes, he's told her a thousand times he's sorry. And you can bet the family china he means every word of it. But the man who allows himself the luxury of any sadistic remark is headed for trouble. Big trouble. Plus a big repair job.

"Sadism," according to the dictionary, is "cruel abuse of others." And is there anything more cruel than hurling hurtful words at any person's "impossibles"? To which there is only one answer:

"No.

"Absolutely not.

"Never."

He who guards his mouth and his tongue
keeps himself from trouble.
PROVERBS 21:23, NAB

TWENTY-THREE

The Right Words at the Right Time

❦

Let your conversation be always full of grace,
seasoned with salt, so that you may know
how to answer everyone.
COLOSSIANS 4:6, NIV

*B*lessed are the merciful,
for they will be shown mercy.

MATTHEW 5:7, NIV

"What can I say to comfort people?" This is a question people often ask of their minister. When friends lose loved ones; when somebody is suffering; when life gets hard; how can we bring a blessing with our words?

During my early years as a pastor, I studied books on pastoral visitation. I attended seminars on ministering to special needs. Like other young seminary graduates, I focused hard on "how to" and "how not to." I learned from the experts, memorized Scripture, experimented with various approaches.

Then finally I came on one answer I could hardly believe. There was an accident in our parish, and I went frequently to the hospital. It was awful, really awful. A twelve-year-old life hung in the balance for days. Finally, we turned that wonderful corner when the doctor said, "The crisis is past. I believe he'll recover!"

One day, after the patient returned home, I went for a check-up visit. My young friend was obviously much improved and thoroughly occupied with the television. So now his mother and I could review the trauma with a good sharing session. Together we went back down our valley of shadow. We discussed some of the lowlights and trudged once more through the dark days of waiting. Then she said something I needed to hear.

"Do you know," she began, "last night we were talking at dinner about all those times you came to see us. We've always loved our pastors, but we'll love you especially for this one thing you said."

Naturally I waited in high anticipation. Was it some Scripture passage? A pensive theological concept? One of my favorite quotes from the mystics?

Would you believe? This is what the lady told me:

"Our family all agreed what helped us most was when you obviously ran out of pastoral words, and you said, *'Gee, it's tough, isn't it? So tough.'* There is no way you could know what a blessing that was. Why? Because it was exactly what we were feeling too."

❧

I'm not sure what the experts would say to this. Someday I'll check it with my friends who are skilled in hospital visitation. But that day I learned for sure: Sometimes the best thing to share is the awful agony on our heart.

Awesome fact, isn't it?
Maybe what the suffering need
to let them know
we really love them
is our plain-vanilla feeling,
such as,
"GEE, IT'S TOUGH, ISN'T IT? SO TOUGH."

TWENTY-FOUR

The Neighbors Are Watching

You are the light of the world. A city on a hill cannot be hidden. Neither do people light a lamp and put it under a bowl. Instead they put it on its stand, and it gives light to everyone in the house....

MATTHEW 5:14-15, NIV

In the same way, let your light shine before men,
that they may see your good deeds
and praise your Father in heaven.

Walter and Beth didn't even realize they were doing it. They were saving a neighbor's marriage, and how I know is that their neighbor told me.

This particular couple lived three doors down. Things were in a real snafu at their house, and several times they almost called it quits. But there was this one ray of hope. Here's how they put it:

❧

"We live down the street from Walter and Beth, so we're together a lot. You know, neighborhood barbecues, bridge, ball games—like that. The thing about them is that they make you feel so good. They always seem to have so much fun with each other. We both agreed love like theirs would be the greatest. We would see them standing there in the door, waving goodnight, and that always sent us back home determined to try once more. So we would start over and finally we began to feel a little improvement. Now things are so much better you wouldn't believe it. Thank God for Walter and Beth. We'd never have made it without them."

❧

Everywhere today there are husbands and wives living lives of quiet desperation. Sometimes it's behind closed doors, sometimes it isn't so quiet. But whether it's open conflict or a silent war, it's a sad fact. Up and down almost any street, dozens of marriages are in bad shape.

Question: Is somebody watching *us*? And will they be helped or hindered by what they observe at our house? Is there a couple in your group whose only hope is to *see* love in action? Reading books, attending courses, hearing lectures, even visiting marriage counselors can be a real plus. But are these really as effective as one living demonstration of how life *can* be together?

Drop one pebble in a stream and what happens? They say those ripples never quit until the pebbles reach the bottom of the stream. Somebody watching us does what we've done, and that affects another person. Then others react to their actions. And who knows where it ends?

This is an awesome realization, isn't it? Our Creator did this to us—by our actions we *do* have a positive or negative effect on other people. Maybe that's what the Bible wants us to realize when it says, "Show yourself in all respects a model of good deeds."

In *all* respects?
Did you really mean this, Lord?
The people I know?
The ones I don't know?
Really?
In *all* respects?
I should be
A model of good deeds?

But he who does the truth comes to the
light, that his deeds may be clearly seen,
that they have been done in God.
JOHN 3:21, NAB

TWENTY-FIVE

What Kids Want Most

A new command I give you: Love one another. As I have loved you, so you must love one another. By this all men will know that you are my disciples, if you love one another.

JOHN 13:34-35, NIV

Drink water from your own cistern,
running water from your own well....
May your fountain be blessed,
and may you rejoice in the wife of your youth.
A loving doe, a graceful deer—
May her breasts satisfy you always,
May you ever be captivated by her love.

PROVERBS 5:15, 18-19, NIV

Straight from my psychiatrist friends. For training in true love, nothing is ever more effective than Exhibit A. If mother and father love each other, and the children know it, that's absolutely the best.

With this in mind, I asked a group of boys and girls to write some essays. The theme would be, "What Makes You Feel Good About Your Parents?"

A few selected answers:

"Sometimes in the evenings I watch my folks look at each other across the room. It is like my father was telling my mother a secret, and she looks back like she knows what he means. They don't do this all the time, but when they do I feel all warm inside."

"It makes me feel good when my dad goes on a trip which he travels a lot and he calls up long distance, and the way my mother comes running, you would think she hadn't heard from him in weeks and you know he only went two days ago. You would also think it was the President or something. I don't think she would care that much if it was the President. She gets happy all over and I like that."

"Sometimes my father and mother get all dressed up together and they go out for dinner. They don't take company along or anything, and he holds the car door for her and she sits beside him close. You would think they were in high school. This makes me feel good."

"My mother doesn't boss my dad around the way Stephanie's mother bosses hers. When my dad says, 'I'm going to play golf,' she just says, 'Have a good game, dear' even when the yard needs mowing and he promised to. I think in home life you have to let some things go, and because my mother treats him this way, my father thinks she is neat. I like this about my parents."

"My bedroom is next to my folks', and I can hear them talking and laughing in their room after we all go to bed. Sometimes my dad sings to my mom, and it sounds awful because he can't really sing. But you can tell she enjoys it just fine. It makes me feel good when I know they are feeling good like that together."

"My mother keeps a cookie jar in the kitchen, and we can help ourselves whenever we want to except right before meals. My dad helps himself too when he comes home from the office, and she doesn't scold him even if it is dinnertime. He always brags and says what a good cook she is. Then she turns around and they kiss. You would think they just got married or something. This makes me feel good."

🌺

Interesting, isn't it, in all their reasons, the message does not come first by words? It's looks, touches, smiles, gestures.

Right on target to the old adage:

"Character is not so much taught as it is caught."
Amazing thought for fathers and mothers:
One way to raise children who
know how to really love
is for us to be Exhibit A
of love at its beautiful best.

TWENTY-SIX

The Freedom to Become

Shall we go on sinning so that grace may increase?
By no means! We died to sin.
How can we live in it any longer?
ROMANS 6:1-2, NIV

Live as free men, yet without using your freedom as a pretext for evil; but live as servants of God.

1 PETER 2:16

On July 4, 1776, fifty-six men made a daring decision. Together they said, "We will no longer take orders from our former authority. We have now reached a maturity whereby we intend to govern ourselves." So, in a dramatic moment, they each signed their names to one single piece of paper.

These fifty-six men did not know how effective their paper would be. Would it actually bring freedom to the little group they represented? Would this signing of their names mean they might hang?

"Yes," they said, "we know the possible cost, *but even so we sign it anyway.* The time has come for someone to declare our freedom. We are a new country. A new people. Here and for all time is our DECLARATION OF INDEPENDENCE."

One year the paper I was writing for did an interesting survey. On July 4 they sent their reporters out to gather information. They visited children's playgrounds and talked to the young. To senior citizen picnics they went. To family events, anywhere, everywhere, they asked this question—"What does Independence Day mean to you?"

The answers? Fascinating. Unbelievable. Scary.

From a rugged truck driver: "Independence Day is when the boss throws this big picnic, and you get all the free beer you can drink. Last year I got crocked, and my wife was so mad she didn't speak for a week."

A fifteen-year-old boy: "Independence Day is so that Americans will know how neat it is to live in a country where you can do whatever you want."

Ominous? The reporters and publishers thought so. "Haven't

we come to a dangerous mental terrain? A terrain loaded with time bombs. These are the time bombs of liberty gone askew."

To which all history makes answer: "On the plains of civilization bleach the bones of countless millions who declared, 'Me first. Me second. Me third. And if there's anything left, I'll take that too.'"

Yes, ominous. Ominous for us as a nation. Ominous for you and me as individuals. Ominous because always and forever the Divine law stands:

Independence does not now
and never will mean freedom FROM.
First, last, and foremost
freedom at its best means freedom FOR.
For you, for me, yes.
But above all true independence means
freedom for the Lord
to accomplish his eternal purposes through us.

TWENTY-SEVEN

Freedom Isn't Free

Oh, how I love your law!
I meditate on it all day long....
I have kept my feet from every evil path
so that I must obey your word.
PSALMS 119:97, 101, NIV

Everyone who sins is a slave to sin....
If the Son sets you free, you will be free indeed.

JOHN 8:34, 36, NIV

A teenage friend of mine learned one big lesson recently.

This young lady was tired of being tied down. So? So she slipped out in the night after taking her father's car keys. Then she went for a midnight ride. She happens to be only fourteen and has no driver's license. But she knew a little about driving, and she wanted to be free. And off she went.

Of course, she got caught. The reason she didn't get by with it is that she ran into another car. Unfortunately, it was occupied by a family of five returning home late from an out-of-town visit.

I am glad to report that no one was killed, but a baby was seriously hurt. And that little life hung in the balance for a long time.

My teenage friend was so courageous she went to the hospital and told those parents how sorry she was. She also told them why she had gotten into all this trouble. It was evident to all of us who knew her that she was going through a personal hell. "Would the baby live?" She said it was "just awful" to look into the eyes of those suffering parents. It was "just awful" to face her own parents. It was "just awful" what everybody was saying. It was "just awful" to look in the mirror.

What my young friend learned is that freedom at its highest and safest has some definite restraints.

There is something native in us which seeks emancipation. From infancy up we struggle to express ourselves, to cut loose from the tie-downs, to do as we please.

When it is rightly understood, this drive for more elbow room is one of our great blessings. History is a thrilling story largely because of man's yearning for freedom.

Yet history also makes it plain that liberty cannot be healthy without respect for some rules. Great civilizations have been relegated to the dump heap when they forgot this truth: Freedom does not give us license to do whatever we please.

Do you think America will stand forever? Will this "Land of the Free" be a permanent part of God's eternal plan? The answer is in part a personal answer. It depends on whether I live by the rules.

What is real freedom? Real freedom is loyalty to those laws which are best for the individual, plus best for all, plus best for the God who created us to be free in the right way. In other words, *freedom of the right kind is only freedom to be the right kind of person.*

This must be what the psalmist meant when he said:

"I walk at liberty: for I seek thy precepts!"

*One of the very best ways
to let people know we really love them
is to say, and mean it:
"I'm sorry I hurt you. Please forgive me."*

TWENTY-EIGHT

"Beware Lest
Thou Forget...."

*He has brought down rulers from their thrones
but has lifted up the humble.*
LUKE 1:52, NIV

Beware lest thou forget Jehovah thy God.

DEUTERONOMY 8:11, KJV

Meet Douglas and Mary.

You will find their counterpart in your block, or across the street, or maybe in your own home.

Doug and Mary came from backgrounds where they had very little. They soon decided, after they were engaged, that they would be financially successful above all else. And they made it.

Doug runs an agency for a national line, and as it prospered they were invited into "better" circles. Then they became possessed of another goal. Their families had been socially insignificant back in their home town. This was another taste of new wine. They liked it. So they put in with the fashionable set. Along with this they picked up some new habits. These were habits they would never have chosen themselves. But you know how it is. Certain things are expected in certain circles.

Mary quit her church school class. Bridge, teas, clubs, social obligations, all demanded more of her time. Her life was getting cluttered, and she had to drop something.

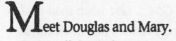

Doug made some changes too. He had always been morally strong and honest to the core. But again you know how it is. New associations call for adjustment.

Then one day Doug was promoted to the top spot.

Since he was moving upstairs he was cleaning out his desk. There to the back of his bottom drawer he came on an old Bible. It had been pushed to a corner, and wasn't that too bad? This was his father's book. Doug opened it for a moment's reflection, and his eye fell on a marked chapter. His father had underlined these words:

Beware lest thou forget Jehovah thy God.... Lest when thou hast eaten and art full, and hast built goodly houses, and dwelt therein.... and thy silver and thy gold is multiplied.... then thine heart be lifted up, and thou forget Jehovah thy God.

SELECTED FROM DEUTERONOMY 8:11-14, (KJV)

You can imagine this whole thing hit him with a terrific wallop. Just that morning he'd been reviewing certain things his company had asked him to do. Some things he didn't like. Such as adjusting certain accounts and touching up their labels. And weren't there other things he'd been liking too much? Such as his new secretary.

What could he do about all this? What he did was to read the verse once more and turn the key in his office door. Behind him. He would go talk it over with Mary.

Mary knew exactly what he meant. This very morning she hadn't been able to get one incident off her mind. Last night after dinner, their four-year-old Rosemary had asked her mother to come outside. Couldn't they sit together awhile on the porch? Watch the kittens play? Look at the sunset?

No big thing. But then again, was it? She'd told her daughter, "Mother is just too busy right now, honey. I have so, so many things to do for the bridge benefit tomorrow."

Then she added, "I can still see those golden curls, shining in the porchlight as she played with the kittens alone. I think I know what you mean, Doug. Let's go talk to Charlie."

So they came, and I thank God it wasn't too late. Some people do catch on in time to start over.

❧

These days Rosemary and her mother sit sometimes and watch the kittens. Doug took Junior to the ball game Saturday. I'm also glad to report that last Sunday the whole family went on a picnic together. *After church.* They even gave up an "important" golf foursome which might have meant something significant to his business.

❧

Really a great verse, isn't it? Worth remembering? It certainly is for me:

Beware lest thou forget Jehovah thy God.
DEUTERONOMY 8:11

❧

Are there some basics
I
need to re-evaluate
in order to let people know
I really love them?

TWENTY-NINE

Debunking the Good Old Days

When I was a child, I talked like a child,
I thought like a child,
I reasoned like a child.
When I became a man,
I put childish ways behind me.
1 CORINTHIANS 13:11, NIV

The Israelites lamented again, "Would that we had meat for food. We remember the fish we used to eat without cost in Egypt, and the cucumbers, the melons, the leeks, the onions, and the garlic. But now we are famished; we see nothing before us but this manna!"

NUMBERS 11:4-6, NAB

Have you ever gone back to the town where you grew up? If you haven't, don't! I did that recently, and it wasn't at all like I remembered.

Shock number one was "the ole' swimmin' hole." How many times have I thought of it through the years? Cool, refreshing, lovely. Today, it looks for all the world like a mud-wallow. Yet what gave me the biggest shock was this constant comment of my aging guide. He's an old man now, and I knew him when I was a boy. Since he volunteered to "take me round," I accepted pronto. But I was almost sorry. Why? Because over and over he repeated this single line: "Hasn't changed one bit, has it? Just like she used to be."

Main street? Can this be the exciting thoroughfare I remember? There was the corner grocery. The big one where I bought all those delicious penny candies. "Just like she used to be?" Oh, no.

Remember the fascinating blacksmith shop? How many hours did I spend watching the smithy mold his horseshoes? Today it's a dirty old place, and my guide says, "Hasn't changed one bit." Can that possibly be true?

"Over there's the town hall?" Really? This little cracker-box building? And here's the village park with its exciting merry-go-round. "Exciting?" The giant slide I've gone roaring down a thousand times in my memory? Had they lowered that too for some reason? "Nope. Just like she was when you lived here."

Then came the clincher. We stood now by the "huge" hill. The one down which we "sped" our sleds those wonderful winter months.

Suddenly the truth came crashing home. The grandeur of my childhood town was all in my head. Those years of "recall" had pumped up the truth completely out of proportion.

Is there one citizen among us who hasn't heard the refrain, "Back in the good old days"? A favorite game, isn't it? Particularly it's a favorite among the de-criers of modern youth. But were yesterday's young really super examples of super parenting?

Recently one of my harbingers of doom came carrying the morning newspaper. "Look here," he said, "vandalism in our junior high again. I remember back in the good old days, kids had respect for authority. For property, too. You remember? Wonder what the world's comin' to. Just awful, isn't it? Plain awful."

What do you think I did? I'm not sure it was the right thing, but I'll feel better if I confess. I went straight to my files and got out a clipping I'd been saving. This is the actual report of an actual happening. I quote:

What a sight chapel presented at prayers this morning. About two hundred panes of glass blown out, the hands of the chapel clock torn off, and the dial pushed in. Front panels of the pulpit gone, the damask between the pillars torn away. On the wall someone had written, "A bone for Old Quin to pick." Old Quin was, of course, the school president.

Time? 1838. Place? Harvard University.

Let's face it. In 1838 or this very year, we have more to do than to pine for yesterday. Be grateful for days gone by, yes. Be glad for good beginnings, certainly. But doesn't there come a time when we must roll up our sleeves and say with the Apostle Paul:

Forgetting what lies behind... I press on.
PHILIPPIANS 3:13-14

THIRTY

Integrity's Reward

❧

Blessed are you when people insult you, persecute you and falsely say all kinds of evil against you because of me. Rejoice and be glad, because great is your reward in heaven.

MATTHEW 5:11-12, NIV

The honesty of the upright guides them;
the faithless are ruined by their duplicity...
The honest man's virtue makes his way straight,
but by his wickedness the wicked man falls.

PROVERBS 11:3, 5, NAB

Justin attended a stag party one night. He went for this reason: he felt that his going would be of benefit to his company. But at the party, some things were going on which didn't suit him. Not even a little.

I wish you could have known Justin. He was very much a he-man: athletic, popular, and fun to know. This was no blue-nosed pilgrim. He never carried a little hatchet to break up bottles or strike down sinners. You wouldn't have found him preaching from a soap box. He simply stood his ground. Quietly. Definitely.

Of course, there were those who made remarks about Justin's "old-fashioned ways." And this night was no exception. Again, no scene. No speech. Justin simply left the party.

Two weeks later Justin's phone rang. It was the vice president of a major American corporation. These were his words: "I've been thinking of you ever since that stag party. Tell you the truth, I didn't know there were folks like you around anymore. I happen to need someone with good, old-fashioned guts right now. Will you come talk with me?"

To cut across that initial contact and several years, this is the scene today: Justin went for a talk, and here he is well up the ladder. Up there where it takes what the phonier called "good, old-fashioned guts."

Encouraging story, isn't it? Some heroic acts, even little ones, do get their reward. But don't we also know this is not true for all people all the way.

Questions for personal pondering:

- How much of a stand do I take when I feel uneasy about the goings-on around me?

- Rather than sacrificing my ideals, am I willing to wait, and if so how long?

- Do I know how to say "No" when I should? And if I must say "No," do I say it the way I should?

- Am I trusting the Lord to bring me, at the right time, to his destiny for me?

PRAYER FOR THE SOMETIMES "NO"

Lord, give me the courage to live up where I think you want me. Share with me the right measure of your courage when you need me to hold firm. And when I must take a stand, may I do it gracefully, lovingly, unless you want me to blow sky high.... help me to do that your way, too. Amen
(MATTHEW 21:12-13; MARK 11:15-17)

THIRTY-ONE

One Strong Effort
Is Worth
One Hundred Intentions

Suppose one of you wants to build a tower. Will he not first sit down and estimate the cost to see if he has enough money to complete it? For if he lays the foundation and is not able to finish it, everyone who sees it will ridicule him, saying, "This fellow began to build and was not able to finish."

LUKE 14:28-30, NIV

In all labor there is profit,
But mere talk leads only to poverty.
The crown of the wise is their riches
But the folly of fools is foolishnes.

PROVERBS 14:23-24, NASB

In the town where I grew up there was one building all of us boys loved. It was a plain old wreck, but we loved it for several reasons. Reason one was that we could see the ball games free. From high up on story six, we had super seats to the pro games. A really super view.

Then as we came to that age when a boy starts thinking, we began asking questions. Whoever started building our beloved old wreck, and why did they give up? It rose several stories, and there was a roof overhead. But no glass to keep out the elements, no doors. Drunkards, lovers, drifters from the railroad tracks, all could enter at their own behest. And they did.

But how did it get this way? One year the curious among us began tracking down some history. Yet with a building so old our findings were only bits and pieces.

Seems that two men had joined hands with big dreams for a garment factory. Then there was an argument with the city over certain specifications. Next, a quarrel between the builders and contractor. His men were loafing, they said, and that brought some lawsuits. So finally, the original planners gave up, settled for bankruptcy, and called it quits.

Today, their dream still stands a shambles. And yes, today it's still the same old haven for drunkards, drifters, and the amorous. Plus pigeons, owls, swallows; they all seem to love it as we did.

Wouldn't it be interesting to know the end of those two men? But maybe not.

One day Jesus was walking and talking with his disciples. "Look," he said, "see that shell of an empty building. This man began to build and was not able to finish." Then he drew a lesson from the shambles (see Luke 14:28-30).

I thank you, Master Teacher, for your plain-vanilla, common-sense reminders. At every step of my life I need to remember: high resolves, noble intentions, dreams, and plans can be a good thing. But what am I doing to see them through?

PRAYER FOR PERSEVERANCE:
Lord, teach me the art of careful planning.
But help me to remember that the worthwhile prizes
are never awarded at the starting line.
In my everyday living,
and especially in things of the spirit,
may I never forget that you said,
"Whoever holds out to the end will be saved." Amen

(See Matthew 10:22, TLB)

THIRTY-TWO

Small Boy and
the Fisherman

❦

Those who go down to the sea in ships,
Who do business on great waters;
They have seen the works of the Lord,
And His wonders in the deep.
PSALMS 107:23-24, NASB

They cried to the Lord in their trouble,
And He brought them out of their distresses.
He caused the storm to be still.
Then they were glad because they were quiet;
So He guided them to their desired haven.

PSALMS 107:28-30, NASB

The small boy did not say a single word. He simply stood there on the deck. Holding his pole. Watching.

Even when the nice man called to him, he merely looked. Not one word.

The nice man was trying out his new fishing equipment. A retirement gift from his employees. They loved him. They'd miss him. So, nothing but the best. A new tackle box, complete with everything any fisherman could wish for.

The nice man was good with children. For years he'd been a Sunday school teacher of children. But this puzzled him. Why did the small boy stand there with his long crooked pole? And why didn't he answer? Was he deaf? Was it that he couldn't talk either?

"Sonny," he called, "can you hear me? Come fish with me. I have some extra string for your pole, and hooks of every kind. Please, let's be friends today. We can have a great time together."

No response. Zero.

So the nice man went on with his fishing. And the small boy simply stood there looking at the river.

Then, suddenly, down river they heard a boat horn. Around the bend, where they couldn't see, there was that loud horn again. This must be a very *large* pleasure boat.

Now the small boy reached in his pocket and pulled out a long piece of cloth. White cloth. Hurriedly he began tying it to his crooked pole. "Poor little boy," the nice man thought as he called again. "Please, sonny, come fish with me. You'll never catch anything with a piece of cloth."

Reaction? Could he believe this? Now the small boy ran to the end of their dock and began waving his homemade flag.

"Oh, no," the man thought to himself, "how very sad. He thinks the boat will stop for him."

Suddenly, the horn sounded three loud blasts. Very loud. Next, unbelievable. The big boat turned and here it came straight for the dock. Then they let down their gangplank, and up the small boy ran.

Into the arms of a big, smiling man he sprang. They laughed. They hugged and laughed some more. Then the man let the small boy down, and turning toward shore he called loud and clear to the nice man:

"Thank you, sir. But you see, you didn't know
the captain of this boat is my father."

It's a solid truth, isn't it?

Every one of us is headed west into the sunset.
"I move this matter be laid on the table
        for later consideration," simply won't do.
When our time comes we must go.
So to let people know they are really loved,
        isn't this the ultimate gift:
Sharing with others our forever and forever faith:
        "The Captain of this boat is our Father."

Daily Affirmations
for Loving People

Question:
How can we let other people know
we really love them?

Answer:
We can't. But we can let the Lord live in us.
And he will let them know
HE really loves them through us.

Forty years ago my Martha and I discovered this secret. We were pastoring an exciting four-thousand-member church. Men, women, boys, girls, old folks, young folks, and the in-betweens. People, people everywhere asking: *Does anybody in this great mass of humanity really love us?*

It's a sad fact, isn't it, that people can get lost even in a church. And the larger the church, the quicker they can get lost. So here was this church of massive proportions that prevented this problem by announcing, "This is a congregation where everyone is prayed for, every day."

I wish you could have known my Martha. Beautiful to look at, beautiful to be with, beautiful to be loved by. And why so? Because when you were with her, around her, or anywhere near her, the same effect. You could feel a very special love coming at you, enfolding you. Real love.

This would be natural, then, wouldn't it? At the center of her soul, Martha heard the Lord say clearly (she often heard him clearly): "There is no way you two can love four thousand people on your own. But if you will let me, I can love them through you."

So we got busy. We prayed together as we never had. We studied prayer. We attended conferences, classes, courses, seminars, and we prayed some more. Out of which came, "Many other churches where everyone is prayed for every day by someone." (Time forbids a follow-up of that miracle here.)

But it takes almost no time to share this one truth again. One single great truth about prayer. One more time:

Real prayer is not something we do. Real prayer is something the Lord does through us. And the thing he does through us is to love with real love. Love divine. All loves excelling.

Yet if you are like we were, or like I am alone, you need help. So here are seven affirmations born out of forty years' experience. In my morning quiet time. In the car, at the office. With people, alone. I use these affirmations for what one of my pensive friends calls, "tuning in upward."

As you read them today I hope you'll say, "I can do better than that for my own tuning in upward." And I hope you will.

In defining "affirmation" most dictionaries use this three-word label: "A solemn declaration." Isn't that exactly what every prayer should be?

> *Lord, I solemnly declare that*
> *every day, Sunday through Saturday,*
> *every morning, noon, and night,*
> *every hour, every minute, every second,*
> *I want you to be living in me*
> > *Building your Kingdom in me*
> > *Loving your world through me.*

Sunday
Affirmation 1

"Who's That Knocking at My Door?"

Would you believe? This is the Lord Jesus himself waiting for my invitation. So, of course, I say, "Come in."

Then what happens? Watch him now. After the meal, he asks for a tour. Such a perfect guest he was at dinner, but now to the bedroom. Look under the rug, under the bed, in the closet, the drawers too.

Living room, kitchen, our little office. Then to the attic and let's open this trunk. The one where we keep our private papers. Oh, no. But why go on? If he's been to your house, you know how it is.

Remember what came next: he asked if he could live here. Take over, run the place, permanently.

PRAYER FOR SUNDAY

Affirmation: Lord, I affirm that I really meant it when I invited you to take over. I do need your help. Especially at loving. Let's try it again, Lord. I want my heart to be your permanent home, that you might live in me and really love through me... really... Amen.

Monday
Affirmation 2

I affirm that every person on earth is a child of God.

In saint and sinner alike, there is a sacred spark that never goes out. My Lord loves them all, and I must.

Yet how can I do that? So many I don't know. Some are plain unlikable. They're odd, they're ugly, they're unpleasant, they're not good company. And I'm to love these too? How can I possibly stretch my preferences that much?

Answer, straight from headquarters:

"Maybe you're trying too hard. Why don't you turn them over to me and let me love them through you? Then they will really know they are really loved."

PRAYER FOR MONDAY

Thank you, Lord, for your mercy. I know you love with an everlasting love, really. Right now, this very minute, take my people-labels and put them away forever. Amen.

Tuesday
Affirmation 3

Today I affirm that prayer peels away differences.

It shows me that other people are like I am. They have wants. They have needs. They hope. They're lonely. They cry.

"Doesn't anyone recognize the worth in me? Just once, please smile at me, laugh with me, be my friend."

Everywhere the same sad song, next verse. At work, at school, at church, over the phone. And now the place of places—*home, family, parents, grandparents, sons, daughters, in-laws.*

The phone in my heart is ringing. "Hello. This is the Lord again. Did you really mean you want my help? One more time I promise you: If you will let me, I will live at your house, in your heart. I will love them through you. Then they'll know they're really loved."

PRAYER FOR TUESDAY
Lord, I really do mean it.
One more time I ask you, please take over again.
Really love through me and at my house.
And oh, yes, Lord, I forgot one thing:
Thanks for needing our home
As a place for you to live and love. Amen.

Wednesday
Affirmation 4

Today I affirm that being someone through whom the Lord loves is a major responsibility.

So I will go deep.... that being I will study to know my weaknesses, my oddities, and how my history shaped me. All these I must bring honestly, openly to my Lord.

Then having faced the negatives, he and I can deal now with my positives; the better me; the parts I'm glad for. This is exciting. He loves these good things, and I can too.

PRAYER FOR WEDNESDAY

Lord, since you've offered to live in me, I hereby put you in full charge of the remodeling process. Before we get back to your original design, some things will need to go. But that's all right. I want to be the best possible person I can be for you to really love through me. Amen.

Thursday
Affirmation 5

Today I affirm that hatred, bitterness, rancor, and ill will must go.

Completely and right now. Jesus said, "If you do not forgive others, then your Father will not forgive the wrongs that you have done" (see Matthew 6:15).

Do you mean, Lord, I cannot be angry for even one moment or two? Or carry a grudge? Or hate one smidgen?

Read it again, Charlie. If he is to really love through you, this is an absolute. You must not soil, nor blunt, nor diminish his love in any way.

PRAYER FOR THURSDAY

Lord, I hear you. Help me to unclutter my life of all my people negatives. Plus my grudges against you; I'd like to be rid of these, too. And while you're helping me there, please school me more in the hard art of apology. Amen.

(If you are thinking Thursday's affirmation is only a follow-up of Wednesday's, that's true. Why? Because to really love others I so often need a double take on loving for the Lord his way.)

Friday
Affirmation 6

Today I affirm that the Lord needs my help with his
nuts and bolts. And that means my money.

Certainly, he loves the whole world. But isn't it true? In our
day, it's a cold hard fact: Some he loves will never hear of him
without funds to get the message through.

Some are hungry. Some need medical attention. And how
many families in the world have no place to label "home"?

"Lord, didn't I hear you say, 'Inasmuch as ye have done it
unto the least of these, ye have done it unto me'"?

PRAYER FOR FRIDAY

*God of the poor, the naked, the needy, let's have another
talk. Let's discuss my giving. I told you I want my heart to
be a channel for you to really love. Now it's your turn. You
tell me today what you want from me in practical help.*

And I will give it.

*Truth is, you gave it all to me in the first place. So use
me now as one who gives by the holy book. Amen.*

Saturday
Affirmation 7

One more time: I affirm that God is love, that he loves his world and everyone in it. Including me.

I believe that he not only loves me, he needs me here to help him.

So what am I to help him do? What does he want from all of us he's left here on earth?

I believe that we are still here to help our Lord with a dream. It's a mammoth dream, a dream he's dreamed from the beginning of time. And this is his dream:

His dream is to establish

A bond of universal love

on which he can build his permanent kingdom

and reign forever.

PRAYER FOR EVERY DAY:

Dear Lord, thank you again for needing me.

Help me to help you with your dream of an everlasting love.

Yes. I really want you to really love through me. Amen.